Learn About Urban Life

Life in a Commercial City

Trudee Romanek

Crabtree Publishing Company
www.crabtreebooks.com

Author: Trudee Romanek
Editor-in-Chief: Lionel Bender
Editors: Simon Adams and Molly Aloian
Proofreader: Adrianna Morganelli
Project coordinator: Kathy Middleton
Photo research: Ben White
Designer and makeup: Ben White
Production coordinator: Amy Salter
Production: Kim Richardson
Prepress technician: Amy Salter
Consultant: Amy Caldera, M.Sc., Elementary School
Publishing Consultant, Writer, and Former Teacher

Main cover photo: Residents mix with tourists in the
famous commercial district Times Square in
mid-town Manhattan.
Inset cover photo: A boy gets help with his homework
on the balcony of the family's apartment in the city.

This book was produced for Crabtree Publishing
Company by Bender Richardson White.

Photographs and reproductions:
© Bigstockphoto.com: pages 1 (C. Penler),
    4 (GreenstockCreative), 13 (J. Group),
    28 (Gary718 H.Shi), 29 (Barsik)
© Dreamstime: cover main image (Gary718);
    cover inset (Orangeline)
© Getty Images: pages 16, 18 (Jon Riley), 19 (AFP), 20, 26
© iStockphoto.com: Headline image (Natalie Helbert),
    pages 5 (Heng Kong Chen), 8 (David Liu),
    12 (Wolfgang Amri), 27 (Scott Lomenzo)
© Topfoto: page 14 (Ullsteinbild)
© www.shutterstock.com: pages 6 (Jeremy Richards),
    7 (Ykm 2008), 9 (Sergio Z), 10 (Gary Blakeley),
    11 (Amy Nichole Harris), 15 (Andrew F. Kazmierski),
    17 (Tomasz Szymanski), 21 (Philip Lange), 22 (Beee),
    23 (Kenneth Summers), 24 (Steve Broer), 25
    (Andrew F. Kazmeirski)

Acknowledgments:
Special thanks to Peter Kszan, resident of New York
City, for verifying information about his city.

Library and Archives Canada Cataloguing in Publication

Romanek, Trudee
    Life in a commercial city / Trudee Romanek.

(Learn about urban life)
Includes index.
ISBN 978-0-7787-7391-7 (bound).--ISBN 978-0-7787-7401-3 (pbk.)

    1. City and town life--Juvenile literature. 2. Central
business districts--Juvenile literature. 3. New York (N.Y.)--
Juvenile literature. I. Title. II. Series: Learn about urban life

HT152.R64 2010   j307.76   C2009-906246-1

5531

Library of Congress Cataloging-in-Publication Data

Romanek, Trudee.
    Life in a commercial city / Trudee Romanek.
        p. cm. -- (Learn about urban life)
    Includes index.
    ISBN 978-0-7787-7401-3 (pbk. : alk. paper) --
ISBN 978-0-7787-7391-7 (reinforced library binding : alk. paper)
    1. City and town life--Juvenile literature. 2. City and town life--
New York--New York--Juvenile literature. 3. Central business
districts--Juvenile literature. 4. New York (N.Y.)--Juvenile
literature. I. Title. II. Series.

HT152.R66 2010
307.76--dc22

2009042421

Crabtree Publishing Company
www.crabtreebooks.com   1-800-387-7650

Printed in the USA/122009/BG20091103

Published in Canada	Published in the United States	Published in the United Kingdom	Published in Australia
Crabtree Publishing	Crabtree Publishing	Crabtree Publishing	Crabtree Publishing
616 Welland Ave.	PMB 59051	Maritime House	386 Mt. Alexander Rd.
St. Catharines, Ontario	350 Fifth Avenue, 59th Floor	Basin Road North, Hove	Ascot Vale (Melbourne)
L2M 5V6	New York, New York 10118	BN41 1WR	VIC 3032

Contents

Urban Areas

Do you live in a **rural** area or an **urban** area? Rural areas are places such as a small town, where few people live. A small town may have just a store, a church, some houses, and farmers' fields. Urban areas are places where many people live. **Cities** and large towns are urban areas. They have more buildings than rural areas. Those buildings are often tall and close together.

▼ Vancouver is one of Canada's largest urban areas. It lies on the west coast of the country. It has many tall buildings in its city center.

Urban areas are busy places made up of many **communities**. A community is a group of people that live, work, and play together. Each urban community has a center with stores, **businesses**, and schools. Houses and apartments surround that center. Beyond these are the **suburbs**—the outer areas of cities. Suburbs are mostly filled with houses.

Everyday Needs

People everywhere need some basic items in order to live. They require food, clean water, and shelter. They need energy to heat their homes and cook their meals. These things are **resources**. In rural communities, most resources are close by. Some families have their own well for water. Nearby farms provide meat, vegetables, milk, and eggs for the town.

▼ A crowded street in Delhi, India. It can sometimes be difficult to provide food, water, and shelter for millions of people living in large cities.

A town with a lot of resources nearby can grow into a city. Many cities are beside lakes that contain fresh water. Other cities are on ocean coasts or near rivers. Items made in the city, called **products**, can be shipped out of the city easily on these waterways. Good links to other cities help urban areas grow and develop.

Airports and railroads are important to large cities. They make it easy for people to travel in and out and for companies to ship products.

Being Big

Sometimes, cities grow quickly. Many people move there to live. The people of a city are called **residents**. The city needs to build enough **neighborhoods** and homes for all of the new residents. It must also build roads to connect these neighborhoods. Residents need to get to places for work, school, and recreation or play.

Highways lead in and out of the big city of Chicago. Thousands of cars and trucks travel along these highways every day.

Together, all the households and businesses in large cities create tons of trash. The trash is often trucked to **landfill** sites like this one.

The city must provide **transportation**, such as buses and subways. These help people move around the city. Urban areas must provide other services, such as lights on the streets, treatment plants to clean the water, and trash collection.

People living in urban areas often come from many different cultures. They need services that help them live in the community, such as help understanding a foreign language.

Districts and Zones

Most cities have their own local **government** to make decisions about the city. A government often divides its city into different **zones**. Cities may have rules about how tall the buildings in each zone can be and what they can be used for. **Residential** zones contain houses and apartments. **Industrial** zones contain **factories** and storage depots. **Commercial** zones hold stores and businesses.

▼ In this photo, the area at the top is an industrial zone. It has warehouses and parking lots. The rest of the community is mostly residential, with houses and trees.

Dividing a city into zones keeps unpleasant things, such as noise and **pollution**, away from where people live. Pollution is the dirty water or air that factories and cars give off. Most residential zones are far from factories, main roads, noisy airports, and from the crowds and traffic of commercial zones. This book looks at life in a commercial zone of a city—in Manhattan, the center of New York City, in the United States.

▲ This busy floating market is near the large urban center of Bangkok, in Thailand. More than eight million people now live, study, and work in this bustling city.

Welcome to New York

New York is one of the world's largest and best-known cities. Some people say New York never sleeps. That is because, day and night, there are stores open and people and traffic on the streets. The center of the city is filled with restaurants, apartments, theaters, and tall, thin buildings called **skyscrapers**. Visitors from around the world come to New York for work and pleasure.

▼ A view of Manhattan, the busiest part of New York. This picture was taken from an aircraft flying over the southern tip of the city.

New York lies on the northeast coast of North America. Two large waterways—the Hudson River and the East River—flow through the city into the Atlantic Ocean.

Traffic fills the streets of New York. The yellow vehicles are taxi cabs. People hire cabs to take them to places within the city or to the airports in the suburbs.

New York is a noisy, crowded city. It has five **boroughs** or parts—Manhattan, Queens, Brooklyn, Staten Island, and the Bronx. Together, they cover an area of 305 square miles (790 sq km). Each borough has many neighborhoods. More than eight million people live in the city. New York is **multicultural**—its people come from many countries with many customs.

Manhattan

New York has a large **harbor**, a place where boats can dock safely. Long ago, many people settled there because of the good harbor.

Today, the borough of Manhattan is known as "the city." New York's commercial zone is in the southern part of Manhattan. It is packed with stores, businesses, and **offices**. The other four boroughs in the city contain more houses, industrial zones, and airports.

By 1885, the city of New York was already an important commercial center. This drawing from that time shows Broadway in the center of Manhattan.

Residents, office workers, and tourists fill the sidewalks in Times Square. This is the center of the entertainment area of Manhattan.

The commercial zone has many skyscrapers filled with thousands of offices. Offices are places where people work together organizing **company** business. Many major banks and insurance companies have an office there. The most important street in the zone is called Wall Street.

Many New Yorkers work in the **financial** district around Wall Street. This area of the commercial zone contains banks and other money-related businesses. The most important business there is the New York Stock Exchange. A **stock exchange** is a building in which people buy and sell money-shares in companies.

These people are stock traders working at the New York Stock Exchange. They keep track of which companies around the world are doing well and which ones are doing poorly.

Manhattan's commercial district is also home to many restaurants, entertainment centers, and stores. People go there to eat, see shows, and buy clothing and other products. Companies in the Garment District design and make many new fashions. The downtown buzzes with workers, shoppers, and tourists visiting some of New York's famous buildings. Residents of the commercial zone live in tall apartment buildings. There are few houses in this area.

▶ Skyscrapers that contain banks, insurance companies, and other businesses dominate the financial district of New York.

In the Office

New York office workers work long days. Most are at their desks by 9:00 a.m. They start by reading email and other messages and looking at their schedules for the day. They work in groups or alone. Most office workers take coffee breaks mid-morning and mid-afternoon and use that time to have meetings with other workers.

▼ Office workers spend much of every day sitting at their desks, looking at computer screens, and discussing business with their co-workers.

For lunch, office workers might eat at the company cafeteria. Many of them leave the office to buy a take-out meal. They bring lunch back to the office to eat while they work. Between 6:00 p.m. and 8:00 p.m., it is time to go home. From bus drivers to street sellers and taxi drivers, office workers see hundreds of people each day.

Many people who work downtown live miles away in Brooklyn or Queens or even across the Hudson River in the state of New Jersey. They must travel into Manhattan to go to work. This is called **commuting**. Each weekday, more than 100,000 workers ride commuter trains downtown to Grand Central Terminal. Some commuters spend an hour getting to work each day and another hour getting home.

▼ Subway and commuter trains are very full in the early morning and late afternoon, when most people are getting to work or going home. There are never enough seats at those busy times.

Buses and cabs are a familiar sight in downtown Manhattan, carrying workers and tourists around the city.

People who live in Manhattan usually ride a subway train or bus to work. Tourists use the subway to visit Manhattan's major tourist spots. Many children in New York take the subway to school, too. Some people in New York own their own cars. Many use them to drive their children to school or to leave the city for holidays.

The government of New York City consists of a large team of people from each of the five boroughs. A person called the mayor is the team's leader. The city government creates new city **laws**, or rules. It decides how the city will spend its money and how people and businesses can use land within the city.

▼ There are more than 35,000 police officers in New York. These officers in Times Square are two of the few who patrol the streets on horseback.

The city government makes important decisions to improve schools and health care. New York's government works to create more jobs and new places for New Yorkers to live. As well, the government makes sure services such as the police department, fire department, street cleaners, and garbage-disposal workers are keeping the city clean and safe.

▼ Firefighters and police officers have an important and difficult job—to keep all of the people living in the big city of New York safe.

Through the Year

New Yorkers celebrate many festivals and special events throughout each year. In March, the city holds its oldest parade, for St. Patrick's Day. On July 4, Independence Day fireworks light up the skies. A New York store called Macy's holds a famous Thanksgiving Day Parade. Millions of people around the world watch the New Year's Eve celebrations in New York's Times Square.

▼ Every November, New York hosts a very long running race called a marathon. More than 40,000 runners race through the streets of the city's five boroughs.

In the summer, tourists and New Yorkers visit the Bronx Zoo, ride the ferry to Staten Island, or walk through Central Park. The cold and snow of winter bring ice skating at the Rockefeller Center and in Central Park. In December, Manhattan glistens with beautiful displays of Christmas lights and decorations. New York City's Chinese New Year celebration is the largest in America.

More people move to New York each year. They move there from all over America and the world. It is a challenge for the city's government to help all the new residents find homes and jobs. New York has many homeless people who live on the streets. The city tries to find or build places for them to live, too.

▼ These workers have offered their time for free to serve food to homeless people. The food was prepared by an organization that helps the homeless.

It takes a lot of energy to light up all the offices in the skyscrapers of New York.

When many people live in one place, they often create a lot of pollution. New York's government works hard to cut down on all forms of pollution. City workers teach residents how to create less trash by separating items that can be **recycled** or changed into something else. The government also looks for ways to use clean **energy** from the wind and the Sun. This energy does not create air pollution.

Commerce Around the World

New York companies do business with companies in other commercial centers around the world. Chicago and Los Angeles are two other places in the United States where commerce is important. London in England and Paris in France are busy commercial cities in Europe. In Asia, there are three large commercial centers—Hong Kong, Singapore, and Tokyo.

▼ This is a picture of London, England. In the foreground is the Tower of London, a 900-year-old castle. Behind it are modern skyscrapers in the commercial zone.

Like New York, each of these cities has a stock exchange. Each of them has a commercial center, too, where financial workers work in offices. The world of commerce keeps growing as people get new ideas and form new companies. Sometimes, a lot of companies fail at once and people lose their jobs. Usually, things get better and the business of commerce, in New York and around the world, starts growing again.

◀ In every commercial center, like this one in Tokyo, there are many stores and restaurants as well as offices.

Many languages
As a major commercial center, New York attracts people from all over the world. Between them, the people who live there speak more than 200 different languages.

Largest store
The world's largest department store is Shinsegae in Busan, South Korea. It contains an eight-story department store as well as an ice rink and movie theater.

Skyscrapers
Skyscrapers are built on a very small piece of land. The Shanghai World Financial Center is one of the tallest buildings in the world. It is 1,600 feet (488 meters) tall.

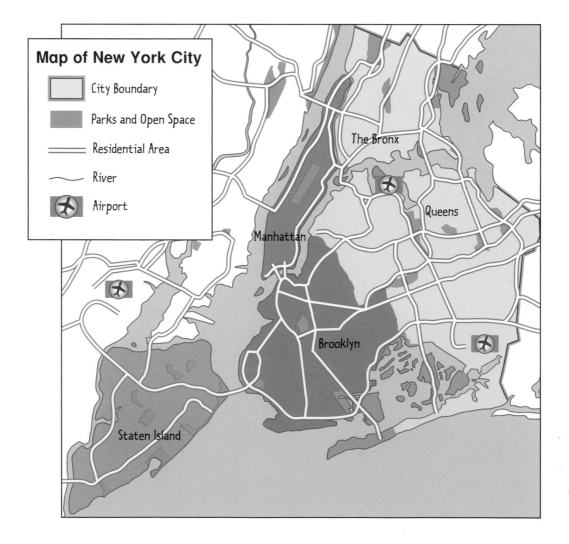

Map of New York City

	City Boundary
	Parks and Open Space
	Residential Area
	River
	Airport

The Bronx

Queens

Manhattan

Brooklyn

Staten Island

Glossary

borough A part of a city

business An organization involved in commerce

city Large urban area, with thousands of people and many houses, offices, roads, and factories

commercial To do with the buying and selling of goods and services

community A group of people who live, work, and play close together

commuting Traveling in and out of a city in order to work

company A group of people who work together to produce something

energy The power to do work, such as heat buildings; energy can come from burning fuels such as coal, or from wind, water, and the Sun

factory A building where people make things

financial Having to do with money

government A group of people who make decisions for a city, country or other area

harbor A sheltered area of water where ships dock

industrial To do with industry or making things

landfill A place where trash is dumped

law A rule made by the government of a country or city

multicultural Made up of people with different customs, traditions, beliefs, and languages

neighborhood A smaller community within a larger area, with its own look and customs

office A place where people work together organizing business

pollution Air or water that contains chemicals or smoke that make it dirty

products Items that are made to be sold to others

recycle To rework a product so that it can be used again

residential An area where people live

residents People who live in a place such as a city or apartment block

resources Things one needs or must have

rural A small, quiet living area in the countryside

skyscraper A very tall, thin building

stock exchange The place where people buy and sell shares in a company

suburb An area on the outskirts of the city

transportation Buses and subways people can ride to get around

urban A built-up area such as a city or big town

zone An area of a city that can be used in a specific way

Further Information

FURTHER READING

Hopkins, Lee Bennett. *City I Love*. Abrams Books for Young Readers, 2009
Loewen, Nancy. *Ups and Downs: A Book About the Stock Market.*
    Picture Window Books, 2005
Pifher, Johnathan. *My First Finance Book.* Alaric Corporation, 2007
Rubbino, Salvatore. *A Walk in New York.* Candlewick, 2009
Thomas, Keltie. *The Kids' Guide to Money Cent$.* Kids Can Press, 2004

WEB SITES
New York
www.pbskids.org/bigapplehistory/index-flash.html
www.factmonster.com/us/slideshow/landmarks-new-york-city.html
www.nycsubway.org/

Banking and Commerce
www.library.thinkquest.org/3088
www.kidsbank.com

Skyscrapers
www.skyscraper.org/WHAT%27S_UP/COOL_STUFF/coolstuff.htm
www.pbs.org/wgbh/buildingbig/skyscraper/index.html

Index